27

Earbud Case 4

Utility Apron 7

Purse Organizers 8

Scented Sachets 12

Hair Adornments 14

Double-Sided Belts 16

Burlap Pencil Roll 18

Vintage Garland 22

Kanzashi Flower Brooch 24

Leafy Pincushion 28

30

2

20

MAKEUP BAG

Use beautifully patterned fabrics to make a simple yet stylish makeup bag. By Eva Moody

YOU WILL NEED

Yardage is based on 43"/44" wide fabric with a usable width of 40".

- 3/8 yd of paisley print fabric for body
- 3/8 yd of solid green fabric for lining
- 3/8 yd of 20" wide heavyweight sew-in interfacing
- 10" zipper
- Sewing machine
- Zipper foot
- Scissors
- Pins
- Thread
- Iron
- Fabric marker

This bag is very spacious thanks to its generous size and will keep your makeup and creams safe. We used heavyweight sew-in interfacing to add a bit more shape to the bag. It is fairly easy to make and once you master this one you can try different sizes. Happy sewing!

TO MAKE

***Note:** Match right sides and raw edges and use a 1/4" seam allowance unless otherwise indicated.*

1. Cut two rectangles 10" x 8" from the body fabric, lining fabric, and interfacing. Baste one piece of interfacing on the wrong side of one body rectangle along all sides. Press 3/8" to the wrong side along one long edge. Repeat with remaining body and interfacing rectangle. Press 3/8" to wrong side on one long ede of lining rectangles.

2. Place the pressed edge of the body, right side up, on the right side of one zipper tape. Place the pressed edge of the lining, right side up, on the wrong side of the same zipper tape; pin. With the body fabric facing up, use a zipper foot to sew 1/8" from the zipper teeth. Close the zipper and repeat for the remaining body and lining.

3. Open the zipper half way. Matching right sides and leaving a 4" opening in the lining for turning, sew the body rectangles together and the lining rectangles together.

4. To box the bottom of the body, match right sides and align side seam with bottom seam; stitch across the corner 1 1/2" from the point. Repeat for remaining corner of body.

5. Turn the body to the wrong side and trim each corner 1/4" from the seams.

6. Repeat Steps 4-5 for the lining.

7. Sew the opening closed. Turn the bag and lining right side out. Place the lining inside the bag; press.

PHOTOS: LAUREL GUILFOYLE

EARBUD CASE

Never be in a tangle again with this handy earbud case.

By Emma Herian

PHOTOS: EMMA NOREN

YOU WILL NEED

Cut from main fabric:

- 1 circle
- 2 half circles
- 1 tab

Cut from lining fabric:

- 1 circle
- 2 half circles

Cut from sew-in interfacing:

- 1 circle
- 2 half circles

- 7" nylon zipper
- Thread
- Sewing machine and a zipper foot
- Tracing paper
- Iron, scissors, and pins

TO MAKE

***Note:** Match right sides and raw edges and use a 1/4" seam allowance unless otherwise indicated.*

1. Trace the patterns (*page 6*) onto tracing paper. Use patterns to cut the pieces as listed above.
2. Place one of the lining half circles right side up. Place the zipper right side up on top so that the edges are aligned (*image 1*). Place one main fabric half circle and one interfacing half circle wrong side up on the zipper. Pin in place.
3. With the zipper foot attached to the sewing machine, sew a 1/4" seam allowance along the length (*image 2*). Fold right side out; press.
4. Repeat Step 3 with the remaining half circles, aligning edges to create a circle. Fold right side out and press.
5. Using a zipper foot, topstitch along each side of the zipper.
6. Open the zipper part way and sewing by hand, baste across the end so that the zipper will stay closed (*image 3*).
7. To make the tab, match wrong sides and press tab in half; unfold. Press long edges to meet the center crease. Refold and press again. Using a regular presser foot, topstitch along each long edge of the tab.
8. Fold the tab in half. Aligning the raw edges, place the tab over the zipper. Using the sewing machine, sew across the raw edges of the tab 1/8" from raw edges (*image 4*).

1

2

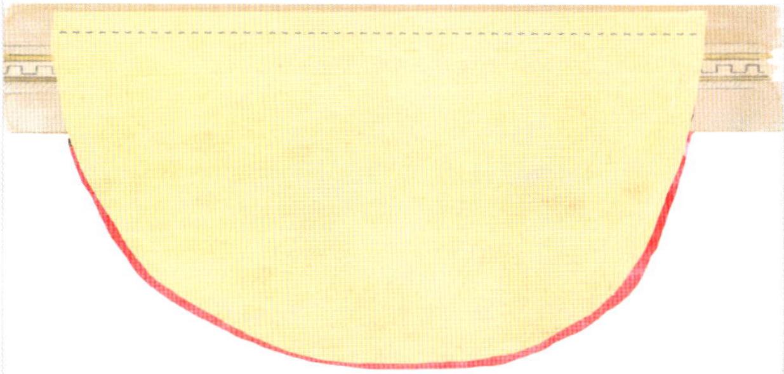

3

4

ILLUSTRATIONS: KELLIE BLACK

9 Place the remaining fabric circle right side down on top of what you have made and place the interfacing circle on top of that. Place the lining circle right side up on the top; pin all layers together.

10 Sew all the way around the circle, stitching slowly over the zipper ends.

11 Trim the zipper ends and any stray threads. Clip the seam allowances and turn the case right side out (*image 5*). Place the lining inside the case.

12 Starting near the tab, topstitch around the outside edge of the circle (*image 6*).

5

6

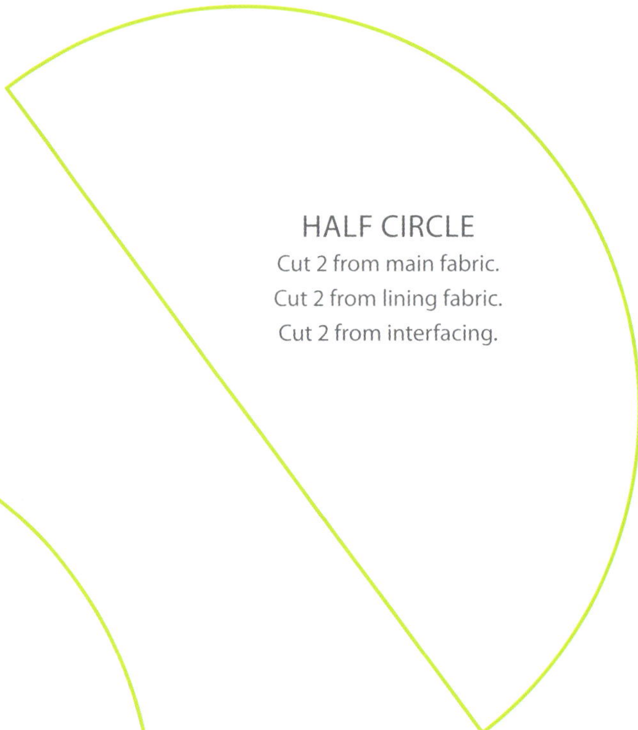

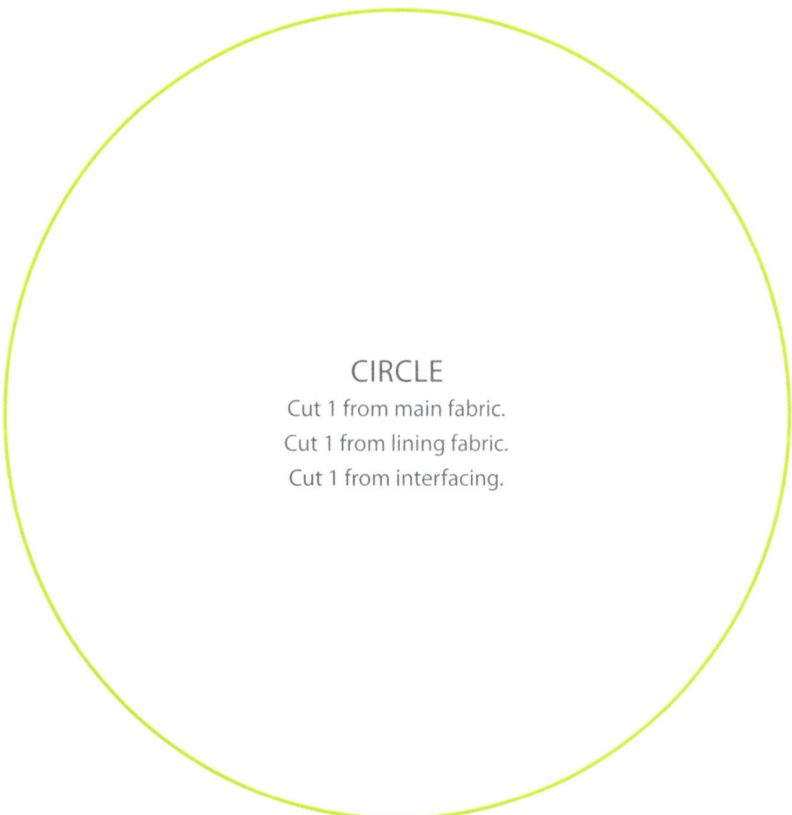

UTILITY APRON

Be the hostess with the mostest in this quick and easy apron by Suzanne Rowland

YOU WILL NEED

- 18" x 23" piece of medium weight print fabric
- 1" wide cotton twill tape to tie in a bow around your waist (measure your waist and triple it to get the right amount)
- Thread to match
- Sewing machine
- Iron, scissors, and pins

TO MAKE

Note: *Match right sides and raw edges and use a 1/4" seam allowance unless otherwise indicated.*

1. To hem pocket, press one short edge (top, if using directional fabric) of the fabric 1/4" to wrong side; press 1/4" to wrong side again. Topstitch in place.

2. Fold the hemmed edge 9 7/8" to the right side. Fold the remaining short edge 1 1/4" to the right side. Sew along each side; clip corners. Turn right side out; press.

3. To make two pockets, sew a line of stitching through the center of the pocket.

4. Matching the centers, pin the twill tape 3/8" from the top of the apron so that it covers the raw edge of the fabric. Stitch along each side of the twill tape being careful not to catch the top of the pocket.

5. Tie around your waist with a bow at the front.

PHOTO: LAUREL GUILFOYLE

PURSE ORGANIZERS

Knock your handbag into shape with a handy organizer.
By Emma Herian

MAIN PHOTOS: EMMA NOREN; ILLUSTRATIONS: KELLIE BLACK

BAG-STYLE ORGANIZER

YOU WILL NEED

Yardage is based on 43"/44" wide fabric with a usable width of 40".

Fabric

$^{1}/_{2}$ yd of polka dot fabric for body

- two $14^{1}/_{4}$" x 8" pieces for body
- four $10^{1}/_{4}$" x $4^{3}/_{4}$" pieces for pockets

$^{1}/_{2}$ yd of pink print fabric for lining

- two $14^{1}/_{4}$" x 8" pieces for body linings
- four $10^{1}/_{4}$" x $4^{3}/_{4}$" pieces for pocket linings
- two $2^{1}/_{2}$" x 8" pieces of fabric for loops

$^{3}/_{4}$ yd of 20" wide heavyweight fusible interfacing

- two $14^{1}/_{4}$" x 8" pieces for body
- four $10^{1}/_{4}$" x $4^{3}/_{4}$" pieces for pockets

Extra

- Split ring for key ring (optional)
- Thread, sewing machine, scissors, pins, and an iron

TO MAKE

***Note:** Match right sides and raw edges and use a $^{1}/_{4}$" seam allowance unless otherwise indicated.*

1 To make one pocket, fuse one interfacing pocket to the wrong side one lining pocket. Place one outside pocket and interfaced pocket together; pin. Leaving one long side open, sew pieces together. Clip corners and turn the pocket right side out. Press raw edges $^{1}/_{4}$" to wrong side. Topstitch the open edge closed with a contrasting thread. Repeat for the remaining three pockets.

2 To make one body, center one pocket, body fabric facing up and topstitched edge at top, on right side of one body rectangle 2" from the bottom; pin (*image 1*). Sew along three sides, leaving the top open. Repeat with remaining body piece and pocket.

3 Lay one body flat and position desired items on the pocket (*image 2*). Pin where you would like dividers. Sew lines where the pins are placed (*image 3*). Pull threads to wrong side and knot. Repeat for remaining outer body and pocket.

4 Fuse one interfacing body to the wrong side of each body lining. Repeat Steps 2-3 to sew pockets to body linings.

5 Sew the bodies together, leaving the top open. Press the seam allowances open. Repeat with the body linings, leaving the top open and a 4" opening along the bottom.

6 To box the bottom of the body, match right sides and align side seam with bottom seam; stitch across the corner $2^{3}/_{4}$" from the point (*image 4*). Repeat for remaining corners of body and lining.

7 To make each loop, match wrong sides and long raw edges and press loop in half; unfold. Press long edges to meet the center crease. Refold and press again. Topstitch along long edges of the loop.

8 Matching raw edges, place one loop on the right side of the body at each seam; baste in place.

9 Turn lining wrong side out. Turn outer body right side out. Matching right sides, place the body inside the lining. Stitch around the top edge.

10 Turn the bag right side out through the opening. Stitch the opening closed; press. Topstitch around the top. If desired, place a split ring on one of the loops.

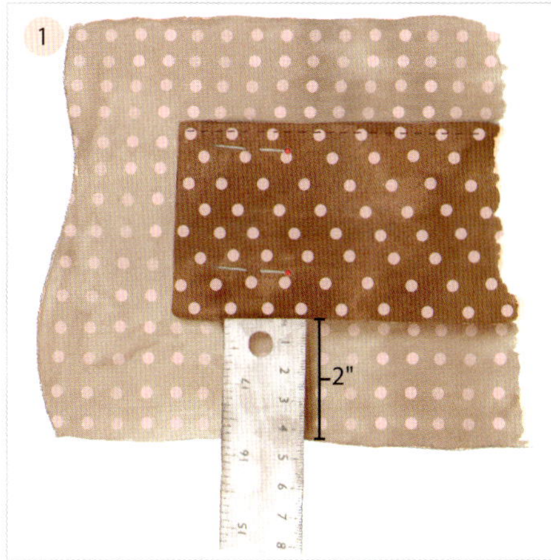

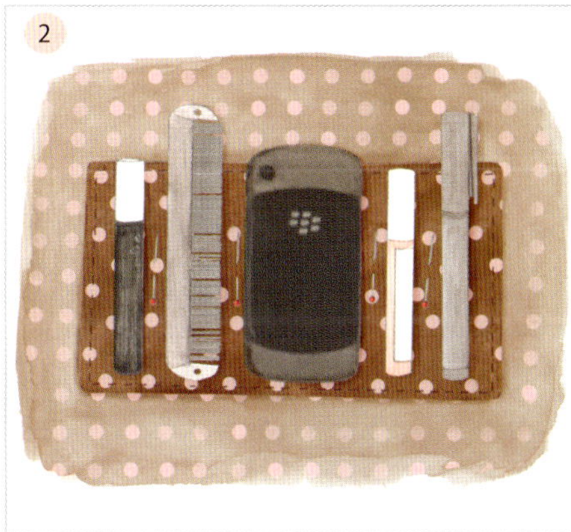

WRAP-STYLE ORGANIZER
YOU WILL NEED

Yardage is based on 43"/44" wide fabric with a usable width of 40".

Fabric

⅜ yd of printed cotton fabric for body

- 27½" x 11" rectangle of fabric for body
- 12" x 4" rectangle of fabric for loop

⅜ yd of purple solid cotton fabric for lining

- 27½" x 11" rectangle of fabric for lining

⅞ yd of 20" wide heavyweight fusible interfacing

- 27½" x 11" rectangle

Extra

- Split ring for key ring (optional)
- Thread, sewing machine, scissors, pins, and an iron

1

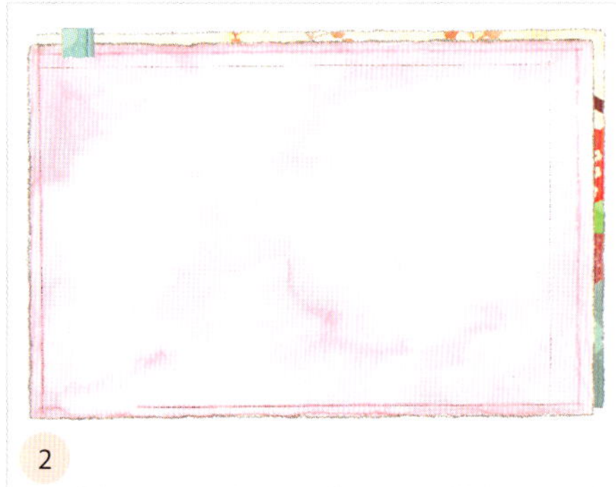
2

TO MAKE

***Note:** Match right sides and raw edges and use a ¼" seam allowance unless otherwise indicated.*

1 Fuse interfacing rectangle to wrong side of lining rectangle.

2 To make the loop, match wrong sides and long raw edges and press loop in half; unfold. Press long edges to meet the center crease. Refold and press again. Topstitch along each long edge of the loop.

3 Pin raw edges of loop on the right side of the body rectangle ⅞" from the top left corner. Matching right sides, place the lining on top (*image 1*).

4 Sew the body and lining together, leaving a 4" opening along the bottom (*image 2*).

5 Clip the corners and turn the fabric right side out through the opening; push out the corners. Sew the opening closed; press. Topstitch all the way around the rectangle.

6 To make the pockets, fold the bottom edge 4" toward the lining; stitch along each side to make pocket (*image 3*). To create the dividers, position desired items and place a pin in between each one. Allow a little extra "wiggle" room (*image 4*). Sew vertical lines where the pins are placed. Pull the threads to the lining side and knot (*image 5*).

7 Add a split ring to the loop if desired.

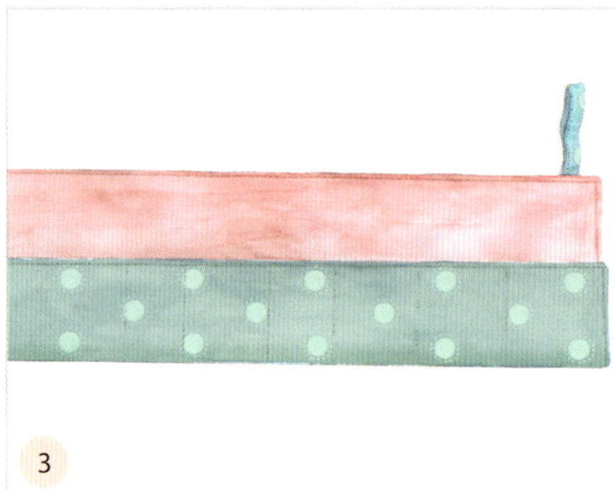
3

4

5

TIPS

- Always backstitch at either end of stitching for extra strength and pull the threads to the wrong side of fabric and knot.
- Always press the edges flat for a crisp clean look.
- Make the wrap-style organizer as long as you need depending on how many items you want to fill it with.

SCENTED SACHETS

This quick project by Francine Kay uses fabric scraps, ribbons and flowers to make sachets that have an air of old-fashioned romance and nostalgia while keeping your drawers sweet-smelling and free of moths. You can hang them together in groups, place them around your house, or tuck them into folded laundry.

YOU WILL NEED

- Fabric scraps (must be thin enough to allow the lavender scent to escape)
- Polyester fiberfill
- Dried lavender buds
- Ribbon - desired length
- Fabric flowers and trims to decorate
- Scissors
- Pins
- Needle and thread
- Tracing paper
- Pencil
- Sewing machine
- Iron

TO MAKE

Note: *Match right sides and raw edges and use a 1/4" seam allowance unless otherwise indicated.*

1. Trace heart pattern onto tracing paper. The pattern can be enlarged to any size desired.

2. Use pattern to cut two heart shapes from fabric.

3. Matching raw edges, pin one end of the ribbon at the "V" of one heart. With the ribbon gathered inside the heart, sew two hearts together, leaving a small opening at one side for turning. Clip point and curves. Turn the heart right side out; press.

4. Fill the heart with lavender and fiberfill; sew the opening closed.

5. Sew desired flowers and trims to the heart.

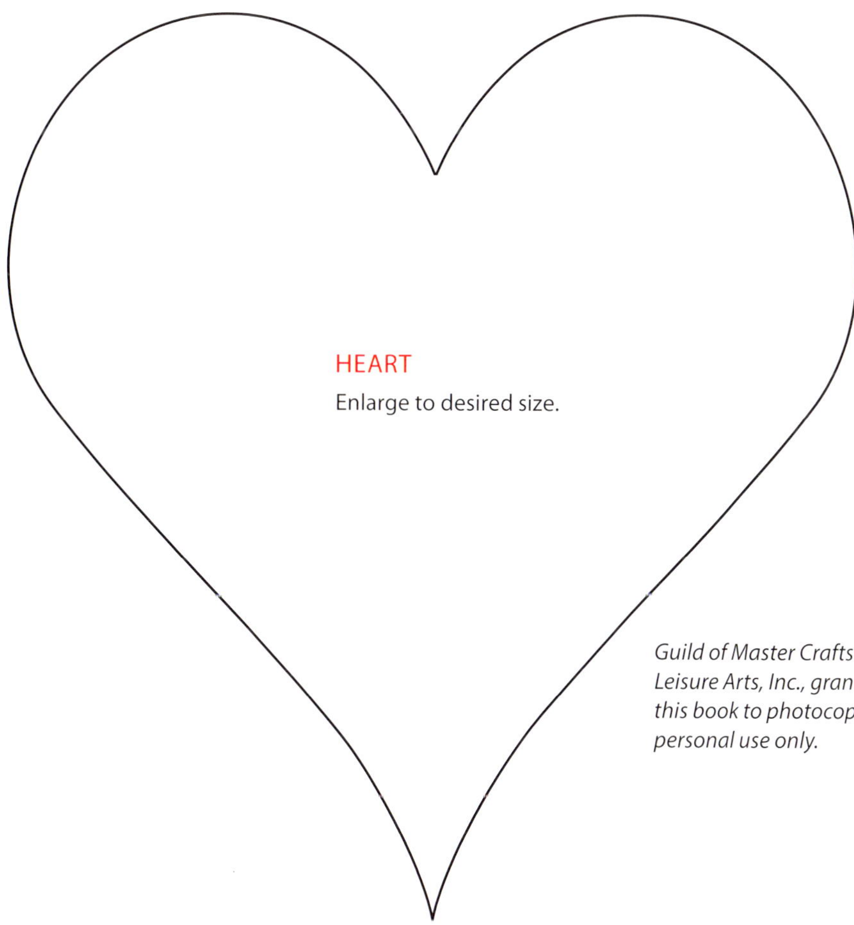

TIPS

- As an alternative to lavender, you could fill your sachet with dried rose petals. Or try mixing rose and lavender together for a really gorgeous scent.
- Chamomile has a delicate fragrance that also complements lavender.
- Another alternative is to use dried spearmint leaves or lemon verbena to fragrance your sachets.

HAIR ADORNMENTS

Bring out your inner Rapunzel with beautiful hair barrettes. By Emma Herian

TIPS

- Practice singeing the fabrics to get an idea of how each one burns; they will give different results. For example, some will puff and others will curl.
- Mix the fabrics when assembling the flower; you will get fantastic contrasting colors and textures.

YOU WILL NEED

Yardage is based on 43"/44" wide fabric with a usable width of 40".

- Various fabrics such as light satin, chiffon, polyester lining, silk, and organza
- Candle
- Bowl of water
- Needle and thread
- Beads
- Scissors
- Pin backs
- Hair barrettes

1

2

3

TO MAKE

1 Cut circles in various sizes: 4", 3½", 3", 2½" and 1½" diameter from fabric (*image 1*).

2 Making sure you are in a well-ventilated room and have a bowl of water near, light the candle.

3 Carefully hold one circle above the flame so that the heat gradually singes, seals and curls the edges (*image 2*). Repeat with all the circles.

4 Stack the circles from large to small to form the petals of a flower (*image 3*). They can be positioned lopsided or in a uniform manner.

5 Sew a couple of stitches through all the layers. Sew a few beads in the center to cover the stitches; knot the thread at the base of the flower (*image 4*).

6 These flowers can be worn in your hair or as a corsage. Sew a pin back (*image 5*) or a hair barrette (*image 6*) to the back of the flower.

***Note:** Never leave a lit candle unattended.*

PHOTOGRAPHS: EMMA NOREN; STEP PHOTOS: EMMA HERIAN

4

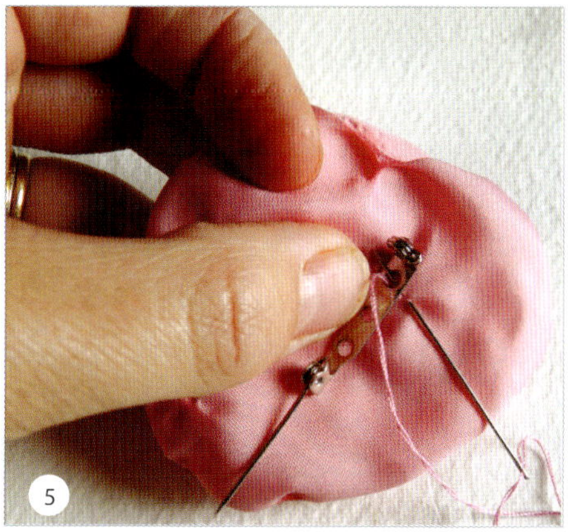

5

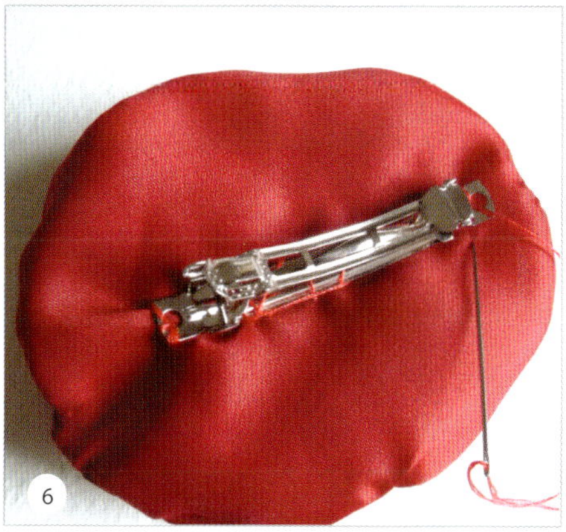

6

DOUBLE-SIDED BELTS

Add a zest of color to any outfit with these zingy citrus double-sided belts; dots one day, stripes the next. What will you choose? By Emma Herian

TIP

- Use stencils if you don't have a steady hand to paint an interesting pattern.

YOU WILL NEED

- 60" of 1" wide twill tape in 2 colors - we used pink and yellow, purple and orange, and turquoise and green
- 1" gold D-rings (2 per belt)
- White opaque fabric paint
- Flat paintbrush
- Pencil with a rubber eraser
- Cardstock
- Wide clear tape
- Paper plate
- Sewing machine and contrasting threads
- Gift wrap tissue paper

TO MAKE

1 To paint dots onto the twill tape, pour a little fabric paint onto a paper plate and stretch one twill tape out in front of you. Dip the eraser end of the pencil into the paint and dab onto the tape (*image 1*). Repeat in a random pattern along the whole length of the tape.

2 Cut a piece of cardstock larger than the width of the twill tape, making sure it has a very straight edge. Cover the straight edge in clear tape to create a wipe-clean surface.

3 For the reverse side of the belt, place cardstock on top of the remaining twill tape. Use the paintbrush to paint a stripe along side of cardstock. Remove the cardstock and wipe it clean. Place it back on the tape about 3/4" from the last stripe. Repeat the paint stroke until the whole length of tape has stripes (*image 2*). Allow the pieces to dry for at least 12 hours.

STEP-BY-STEP PHOTOGRAPHS: EMMA HERIAN

4 Place the ends of the tapes right sides together and sew back and forth 1/2" from end (*image 3*). Turn the belt right side out. At the opposite end, fold in 1" of each tape and pin both tapes together (*image 4*).

5 Because the paint has a rubbery texture, it needs to be sewn between two layers of tissue paper. Cut a long wide strip of tissue paper the length of the belt.

6 Fold the tissue paper in half and sandwich the belt in between; pin in place. Starting from the sewn end, sew all the way down one long edge of the belt, along the unsewn end, and back up the other long edge to where you started (*image 5*). Remove the tissue paper and trim any stray threads.

7 Thread two D-rings on one end of the belt. Fold the end of the tape over 1"; pin (*image 6*).

8 With the edge of the presser foot along the flat side of the D-rings, sew back and forth through all layers; trim any stray threads. Sew a second line of stitching about 3/8" from the first line; trim threads.

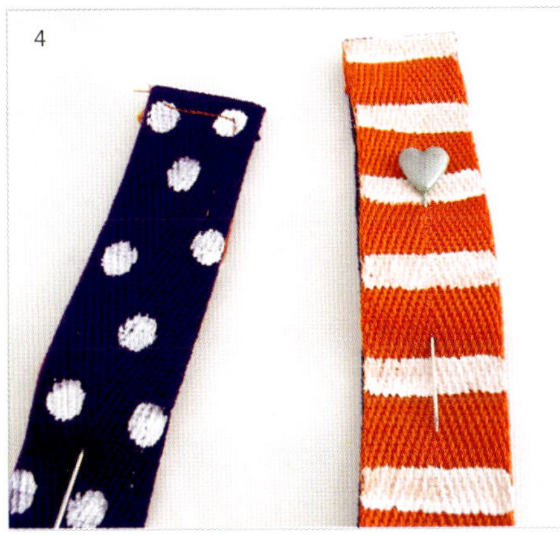

BURLAP PENCIL ROLL

Get your pencils organized with this gorgeous rainbow roll. By Linda Robertus

TIPS

- I used a very loosely woven burlap. If you have a piece of more densely woven fabric, you may need to pull out some fibers to make room for the yarn.
- Burlap frays terribly, so don't cut it until you are ready to start working with it. It also sheds a lot. So don't wear your best clothes and clean your sewing machine afterwards.
- Sewing multiple layers together is easier with a walking foot on your machine.

PHOTOS: EMMA NOREN; STEP PHOTOS: LINDA ROBERTUS

YOU WILL NEED

- 14 1/4" x 13 1/2" piece of burlap fabric
- Two 14 1/4" x 13 1/2" pieces of white solid fabric, one folded in half horizontally
- Tapestry wool yarn: 18" each of red, orange, yellow, green, blue and purple
- 20" of jute twine
- Sewing thread to match burlap
- Darning needle and pins
- Sewing machine
- Scissors, ruler, rotary cutter and cutting mat
- Fabric marker
- Iron

1

2

3

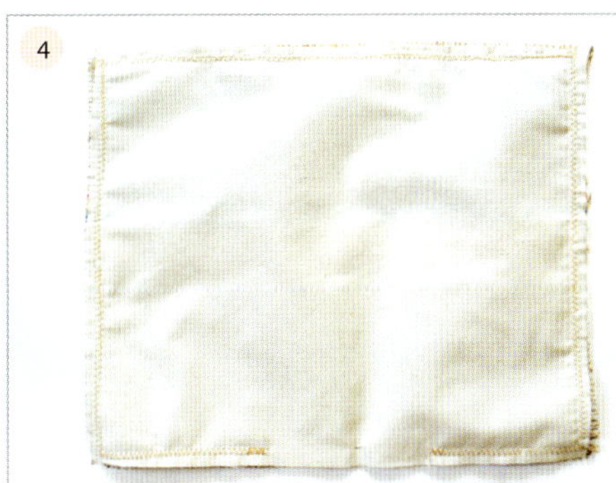
4

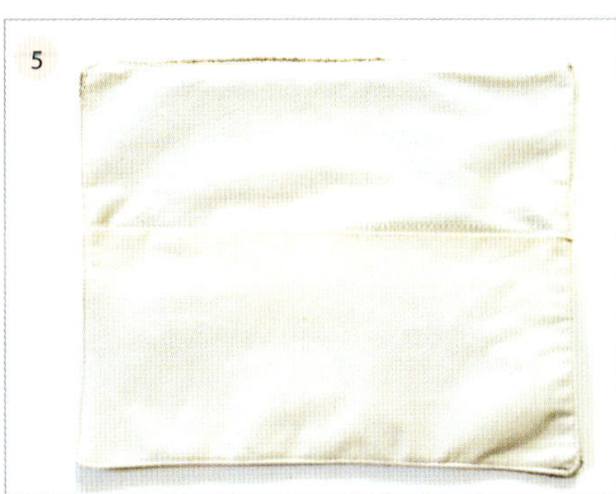
5

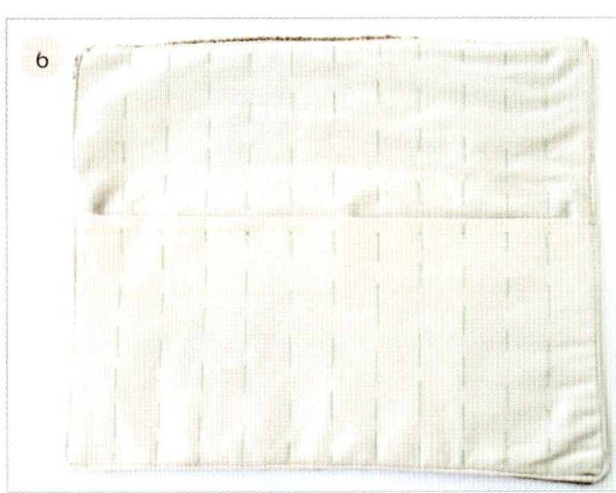
6

TO MAKE

Note: *Match right sides and raw edges and use a 1/4" seam allowance unless otherwise indicated.*

1 Use the needle to weave red tapestry wool through the burlap 4 3/4" from the top long edge; trim the yarn ends. Continue with the orange yarn, followed by the yellow, green, blue and purple yarns (*image 1*). Press the burlap with a hot steam iron.

2 Stack the fabric pieces in the following order (*image 2*): white solid piece, folded white solid piece (aligned at the bottom) and burlap piece (with the yarns nearer the top). Using a rotary cutter and a cutting mat, trim the pieces to 13 1/2" x 11". Pin the outside edges together (*image 3*).

3 Use a wide zigzag stitch and a 1/4" seam allowance to sew around the edges, leaving a 6" opening in the bottom edge (*image 4*). Clip the corners and turn the pencil roll right side out. Push out the corners carefully; press.

4 Topstitch close to all edges, closing the opening (*image 5*).

5 With a fabric marker and a ruler, mark the lines for the pencil pockets. We have 11 lines, about 1" apart (*image 6*). Starting at the bottom edge, stitch these lines, backstitching at beginning and end.

6 Place the pencil roll with the burlap side up. Matching the center of the twine at the center of the right edge of the burlap, stitch back and forth a few times on top of the topstitching to securely fasten the twine.

7 Put your pencils in the pockets, roll up and tie a knot.

SEWING CADDY

Keep your sewing tools neat and tidy with our handy organizer. By Anne Ogden

TIPS

- A fat quarter is a piece of fabric measuring approximately 18" x 21". A fat eighth is half of a fat quarter and measures approximately 18" x $10^{1}/_{2}$".
- When assembling the sewing caddy, it is easier to baste the pockets and pincushion in place, but you can use pins if you prefer.

YOU WILL NEED

- 1 fat quarter of main fabric
- 1 fat quarter of lining fabric
- 1 fat eighth of tightly woven white fabric to make bag for pincushion filling
- Emery or crushed walnut shells for pincushion filling
- $^{3}/_{8}$ yd of 43"/44" wide fabric for binding
- 17" x 19" piece of polyester batting
- Scissors
- Thread in a complementary color
- Sewing machine
- Iron
- Pins

TO MAKE

1 To begin, cut out the fabric as follows:

For the organizer base – cut one $6^{3}/_{4}$" x 19" rectangle each of main fabric, polyester batting, and lining fabric.

Pockets – cut two pieces $6^{3}/_{4}$" x $5^{1}/_{2}$" each of main fabric, polyester batting, and lining fabric.

Pincushion – cut two pieces 7" x $4^{3}/_{4}$" each of main fabric and white fabric.

Binding – cut 1 strip $2^{3}/_{8}$" x 53" (piecing as necessary) and 2 strips $2^{3}/_{8}$" x $6^{3}/_{4}$".

2 Starting with the organizer base, layer the main fabric, polyester batting and lining fabric, making sure the right sides of the fabrics face out (*image 1*). Baste the layers together with random long basting stitches. Repeat with the pockets (*image 2*).

3 To make the pockets, press the two short binding strips in half lengthwise. Place the first binding strip with raw edges aligned and right sides together along the main fabric on the $6\frac{3}{4}$" side of pocket – sew through all layers with a $\frac{1}{4}$" seam allowance (*image 3*).

4 Fold the binding over to the lining side of the pocket and slipstitch into place (*image 4*). Bind the remaining pocket in the same way.

5 To make the bag for the pincushion filling, place white fabric right sides together and sew along the long edges using a $\frac{1}{4}$" seam allowance. Turn right side out. Repeat with the pincushion fabric but also sew along one short end. Turn right side (*image 5*). Fill the bag with emery and sew across the open end. Place the bag of emery into the pincushion and baste across the ends.

6 Assemble the caddy by placing the pockets at either end of the main piece and the pincushion in the middle. Baste the pockets and the pincushion into place (*image 6*).

7 Leave 2" of the binding unsewn and start sewing in the middle of one pocket and work towards the corner. Stop $\frac{1}{4}$" from the corner and backstitch for a few stitches. Cut the thread and take the caddy out of the machine. To miter, fold the binding upwards, aligned with the adjacent edge and then fold down even with the raw edge you have just sewn.

8 Start sewing again along the edge (*image 7*). Continue sewing binding to quilt, stopping approximately 5" from starting point; backstitch.

9 Leaving enough fabric to fold under about $\frac{1}{2}$" (*image 8*), tuck one piece of binding under the other and pin into place before sewing across. Fold the binding to the outside and slipstitch in place.

1

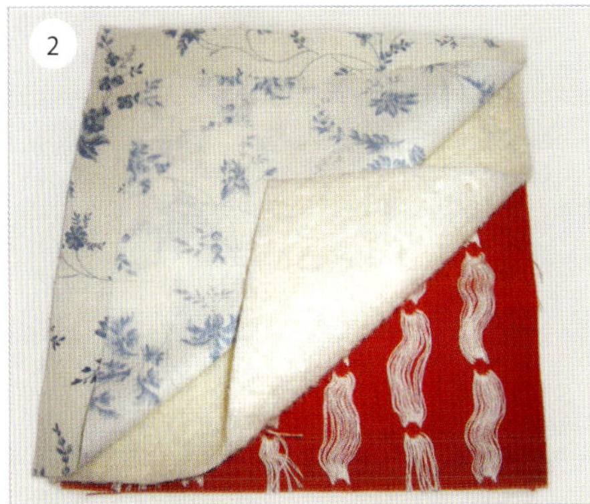
2

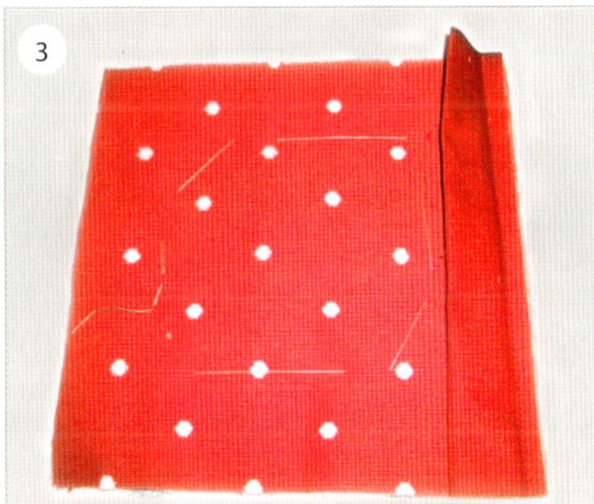
3

4

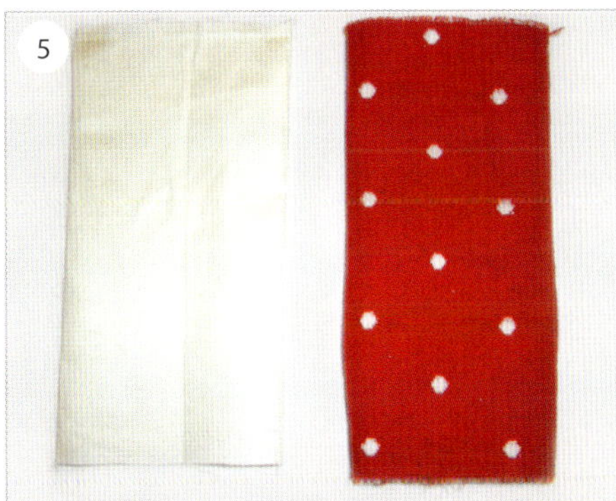
5

6

7

8

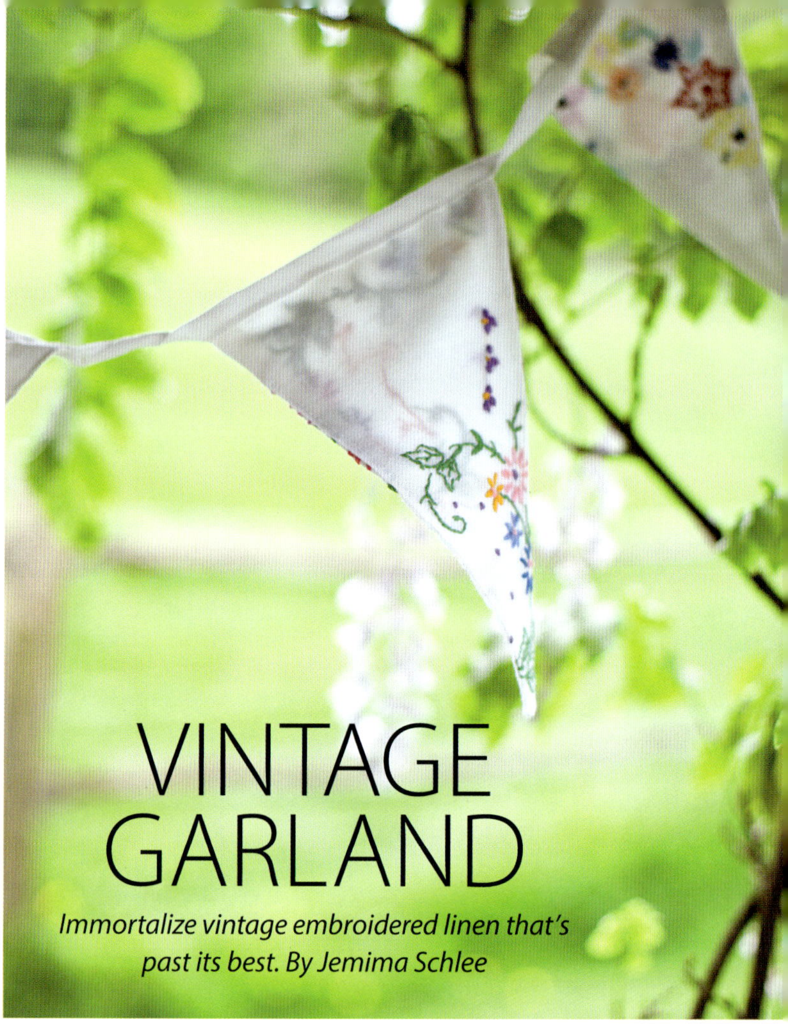

VINTAGE GARLAND

Immortalize vintage embroidered linen that's past its best. By Jemima Schlee

YOU WILL NEED

- Vintage embroidered linens
- 1" wide white twill tape desired length of garland
- Sewing machine
- Threads, sewing needle, iron, and pins
- Scissors
- Iron

TIPS

- This is an excellent way to use old linens that may have become victims of wear and tear or moths.
- Make a quick version of this by sewing the flags from a single thickness of fabric, folding the two long edges over at Step 2 and zigzag stitching along the raw edges to make a hem – or simply cut out with pinking shears. It won't be as sturdy, and probably won't become a family heirloom, but will take you a fraction of the time to make.

TO MAKE

***Note:** Match right sides and raw edges and use a $\frac{1}{4}$" seam allowance unless otherwise indicated.*

1 To make a pattern, draw a triangle on paper or cardstock $6\frac{1}{2}$" wide at the top, tapering down to $9\frac{1}{2}$" long. Use the pattern to cut two triangles for each desired flag from the linens.

2 Backstitching at beginning and end, sew two triangles together along the long edges, pivoting at the point. Trim the seam allowance at the point (*image 1*).

3 Turn the flag right side out; press (*image 2*).

4 Topstitch close to the long edges (*image 3*) If needed, trim along the top of the flag to straighten.

5 Repeat Steps 2-4 to make desired number of flags.

6 To make a loop, press one end of the twill tape over $\frac{1}{4}$". Press folded end over $2\frac{3}{4}$". Stitch a short zigzag stitch to secure the loop (*image 4*). Repeat for the remaining end.

7 Press the tape in half between the two loops.

8 Starting 6" from one loop, place the flags into the fold of the tape; pin in place approximately $2\frac{1}{2}$" apart. Starting at one end, stitch along the open edges of the folded tape from one loop to the other, closing the tape and attaching the flags (*image 5*).

1

2

3

4

5

STEP-BY-STEP PHOTOGRAPHS: JEMIMA SCHLEE

KANZASHI FLOWER BROOCH

Kanzashi are hair ornaments used in traditional Japanese hairstyles; with a little tweaking this pretty flower makes a gorgeous brooch. By Emma Herian

YOU WILL NEED

- Seven $4^3/_4$" x $4^3/_4$" squares and one $1^1/_2$" diameter circle of printed fabric for each brooch
- Iron
- Pins
- Needle and thread
- Buttons
- Pin back
- Fabric glue

TIPS

- Experiment with the number of petals but make sure it's always an odd number.
- For a fun contrast, use different types of fabric for color and texture.

TO MAKE

1 For a rounded tip petal, match wrong sides and press one square in half to form a triangle.

2 With the folded edge facing you, bring the left and right outside corners up to meet the top corner and press (*images 1 and 2*).

3 Turn the diamond shaped fabric over and fold the outside corners into the center so the tips meet (*image 3*). Bring the sides together and fold in half so that the last folds made are now facing each other (*image 4*). Push a pin through the middle making sure to catch all the folds to secure; lay aside.

4 Repeat Steps 1-3 for the remaining six squares of fabric.

STEP-BY-STEP PHOTOGRAPHS: EMMA HERIAN

5 For a pointed tip petal follow Steps 1 and 2. Fold the outside corners into the center so it looks like a kite (*image 5*). Carefully fold in half so that the last two folds are on the outside; pin to hold all the folds (*image 6*).

6 Once all seven petals have been made, trim off the triangles at the raw ends of each petal making sure you keep the pins in.

7 To assemble the petals, double the thread on the needle and knot the end. Thread each petal on where the pin is holding the folds, making sure each petal is facing the same way (*image 7*) Sew again through the first petal pulling the thread taut. You will have a rough flower shape.

8 Tweak each petal into desired position and turn over so you have the back facing you. Bring the needle and thread to the back and sew the petals to each other close to the center (*image 8*). Turn over and repeat the process on the front; knot and trim the thread.

9 Cut a small circle of the same fabric and glue it to the back of the flower to hide the center; allow to dry.

10 To finish the flower, sew a button to the front. Sew a pin back to the back. Pull the petals open a little and place a bit of glue between each. Squeeze the petals together and hold with a pin. Remove the pins when dry.

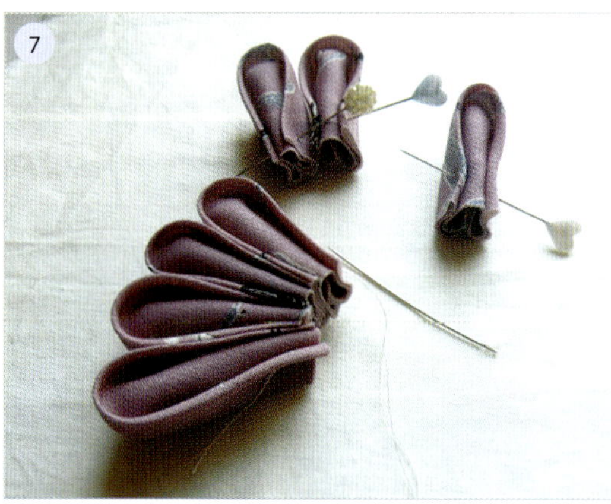

ACCESSORY HANGERS

Accessory hangers are a simple way to store belts, scarves and bags in your closet and a fantastic use for fabric scraps. By Jemima Schlee

FOR EACH HANGER, YOU WILL NEED

- $2^{3}/_{4}$" x 9" scrap of fabric
- 12mm snap
- Shower curtain hook
- Sewing machine
- Snap fastening tool
- Sewing needle and thread
- Scissors
- Iron
- Pins

TO MAKE

***Note:** Match right sides and raw edges and use a $^{1}/_{4}$" seam allowance unless otherwise indicated.*

1 Matching long raw edges, fold strip in half so it measures $1^{3}/_{8}$" x 9". Sew along the long edges leaving a $2^{1}/_{2}$" opening roughly in the middle of the seam.

2 Press the seam allowances open along the center of the tube. Sew across each short end. Clip the corners and turn the strip right side out through the opening; push the corners out. Sew the opening closed and press.

3 Following the manufacturer's instructions, attach the two halves of the snap to the strip $^{5}/_{8}$" from each end.

4 With the wrong side up, fold the bottom end of the strip up 2". Stitch back and forth a few times approximately $^{1}/_{2}$" above the fold, depending on the size of the hook – it needs to be a snug fit. Trim all threads and push the top of the hook through the channel.

LEAFY PINCUSHIONS

Make pretty little leaf pincushions from felt to keep your needles and pins in order.

By Jemima Schlee

YOU WILL NEED

For each pincushion

- Two 4" x 4" squares of felt
- Scraps of contrasting felt for leaves
- Tailor's chalk or air-soluble fabric marking pen
- Pinking shears
- Scissors
- Sewing needle and pins
- Sewing machine
- Assorted color threads
- Polyester fiberfill
- Tracing paper

TO MAKE

1 Trace pattern onto tracing paper. Using the pattern, cut a leaf from a felt scrap. Use tailor's chalk or a marking pen to mark the leaf stitching positions from the pattern (*image 1*).

2 Use a contrasting color thread and a decorative stitch on the sewing machine to stitch the v-shaped "veins" on the leaf (*image 2*).

3 Use pinking shears to cut around the edge of the leaf.

4 Pin the leaf to one of the felt squares along one diagonal. Use a decorative stitch to sew along the center "spine" of the leaf (*image 3*).

5 Place the square with the leaf attached to it on top of the second square, aligning all the edges. Using a contrasting color thread and leaving a $1\frac{1}{2}$" opening, stitch a $\frac{3}{8}$" seam all the way around. Stuff the pincushion with fiberfill through the opening in the seam (*image 4*).

6 Stitch along the opening to close the seam completely. Finally, trim around all four sides of the pincushion with the pinking shears (*image 5*).

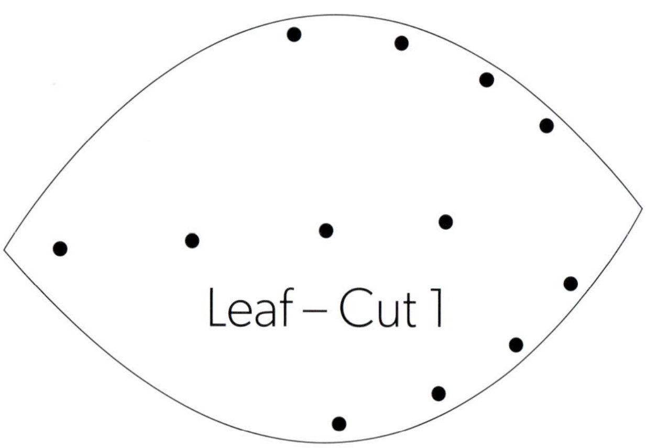

STEP-BY-STEP PHOTOGRAPHS: JEMIMA SCHLEE

TIPS

- Start and finish the stitched V-shapes just inside the edges of the felt leaf at Step 2, leaving enough space for cutting around with the pinking shears at Step 3.

SCISSOR CASE

Inspired by the wings of a crane in flight, the flaps of this scissor case are folded to close the case. By Elizabeth Healey

TIP

- You could use a piece of ribbon as a snap cover, although you might need a longer length to make up the bulk.

YOU WILL NEED

- Two rectangles of fabric 8" x 10" (one for outer fabric and one for lining)
- Two rectangles of fusible interfacing 8" x 10"
- 1" x $8^{3}/_{8}$" strip of fabric (same as used for lining)
- 1 snap
- Sewing machine
- Needle and thread
- Iron, scissors, and pins
- Tracing paper

TO MAKE

***Note:** Match right sides and raw edges and use a $^{1}/_{4}$" seam allowance unless otherwise indicated.*

1 Fuse interfacing to each fabric.

2 Trace pattern (page 32) onto tracing paper; cut out. Pin pattern to outer fabric and cut out; remove pattern. Trim the pattern to the green line on the pattern. Pin pattern to lining fabric and cut out; remove pattern.

3 On the lining fabric, turn a small hem to the wrong side just short of the sewing line for the outer fabric. Miter the point and sew the hem in place (*image 1*).

4 Set your machine to a short stitch length. Sew outer fabric and lining together from blue dot to blue dot along the wings only (*image 2*). Trim the excess fabric at the points, and snip into the "V" where the wings meet.

5 Turn wings right side out and gently push points into sharp tips using a blunt object. Be careful not to push so hard that you bust the seam. When you are happy with the shape, press the wings (*image 3*).

6 Matching right sides and dots, fold outer fabric together to form a cone. Backstitching at the beginning and end and using a $^{1}/_{2}$" seam allowance, sew the edges together. Hand stitch the lining hem to the seam allowance on each side.

7 Turn the entire case right side out. Push the lining into a cone shape; press (*image 4*). Fold the wing on top to the back of the case along the other wing; press. Secure in place with a few stitches. Fold the back wing forward; press (*image 5*).

8 Sew a snap to the inside front wing and body.

9 Match wrong sides and long raw edges and press long strip of fabric in half; unfold. Press long edges to meet the center crease. Refold and press again. Topstitch along each long edge of the strip.

10 To make a snap cover, coil the strip into a disc, securing it with a few stitches. Sew to the front flap to hide any stitches or impression made by the snap (*image 6*).

1

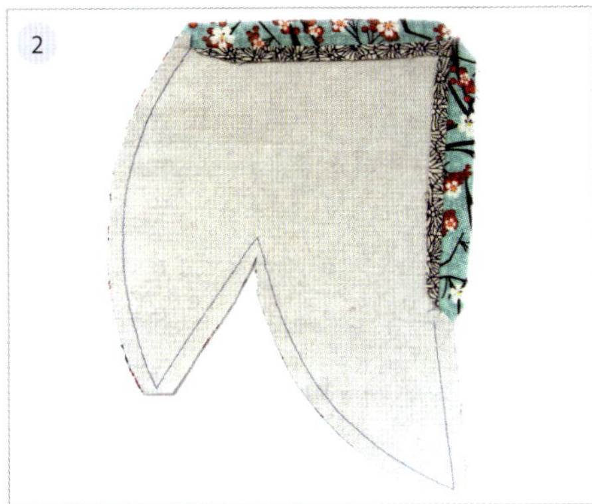
2

3

4

5

6

STEP-BY-STEP PHOTOGRAPHS: ELIZABETH HEALEY

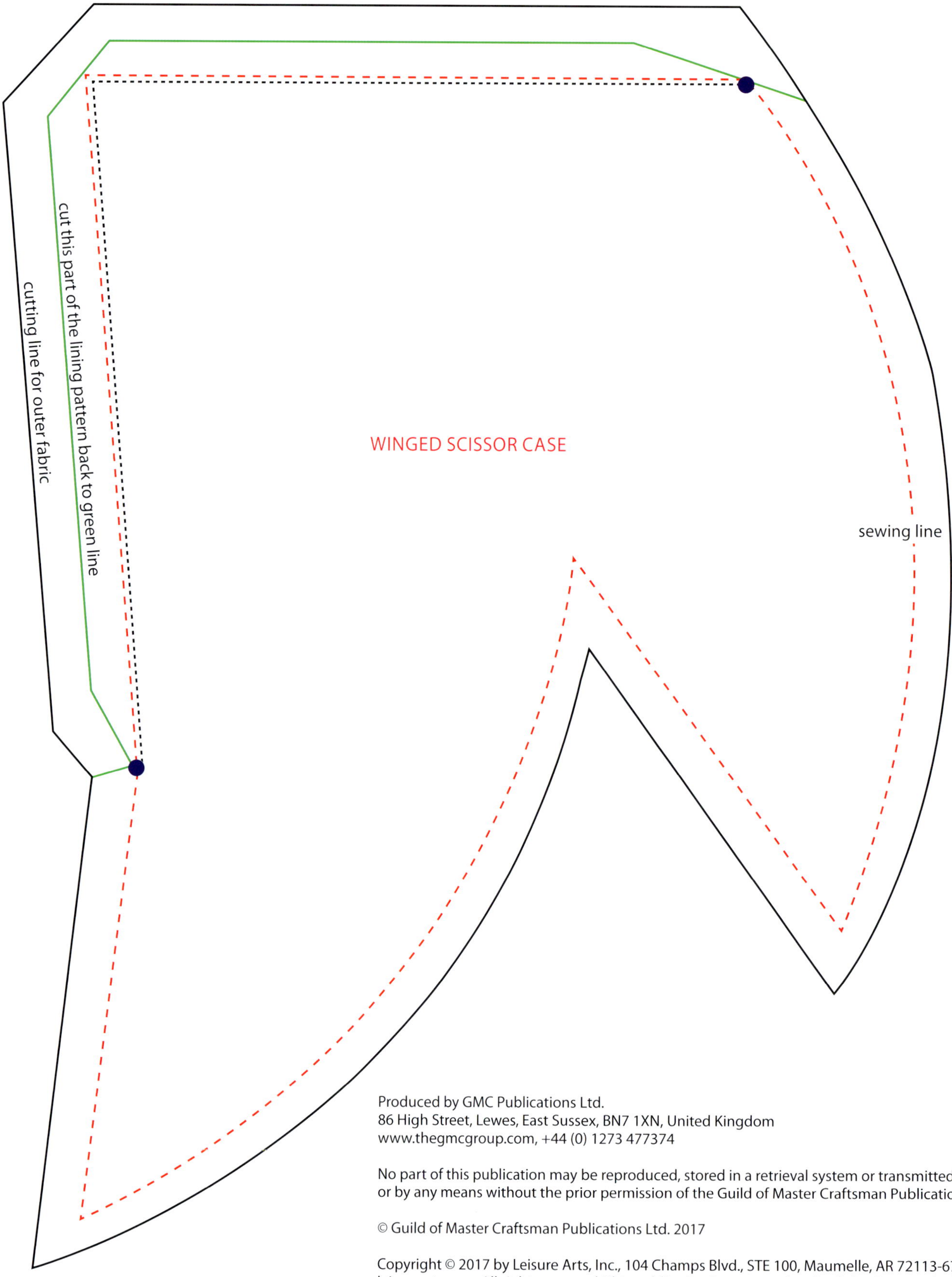

Produced by GMC Publications Ltd.
86 High Street, Lewes, East Sussex, BN7 1XN, United Kingdom
www.thegmcgroup.com, +44 (0) 1273 477374